Dyslexia
How would I cope?

of related interest

A Little Edge of Darkness
A Boy's Triumph Over Dyslexia
Alexander Faludy and Tanya Faludy
ISBN 1 85302 357 4

Check-Mate
A Pocket-Size Guide to Everyday Spellings for Dyslexics
Alan O'Brien
ISBN 1 85302 165 2

Children with Special Needs
Assessment, Law and Practice –
Caught in the Acts, 3rd edition
John Friel
ISBN 1 85302 280 2

Young Adults with Special Needs
Assessment, Law and Practice –
Caught in the Acts
John Friel
ISBN 1 85302 231 4

Dyslexia
How would I cope?

Michael Ryden

Foreword by Derek Copley

Jessica Kingsley Publishers
London and Bristol, Pennsylvania

First published in the United Kingdom in 1989 by
Jessica Kingsley Publishers Ltd
116 Pentonville Road
London N1 9JB, England
and
1900 Frost Road, Suite 101
Bristol, PA 19007, U S A

Second edition 1992
Third edition 1997

Library of Congress Cataloging in Publication Data
A CIP catalogue record for this book
is available from the Library of Congress

British Library Cataloguing in Publication Data
Ryden, Michael, 1960–
Dyselxia : How would I cope?. - 3rd ed.
1. Dyslexia - Popular works 2. Dyslexics
I. Title
616.8′553

ISBN 1 85302 385 X

Printed and Bound in Great Britain by
Biddles Ltd., Guildford and King's Lynn

CONTENTS

PART III – Attitudes, Counselling and Teaching

Appendices

Foreword

I count it a privilege to write the foreword to this book.

I have known the author personally for several years and during that time I have observed his determination to succeed in life despite his disability.

I have worked with several dyslexics over the span of my teaching career but Mike was the first one to enable me to step into his shoes and to see things from inside his personal world. He did this not merely by telling me but by showing me, using the experiments described in Part II. It was a real eye opener, and gave me a new sympathetic understanding.

The world has many disabled people, many of whom have come to terms with their limitations and whose self-esteem is high. Alas the same is not so true of us who meet disadvantaged people from time to time. We simply do not know how to react and our fears cause us to reject them or treat them with less than the dignity they deserve. We do them a disservice, damage their self image and indeed hinder their progress.

Today there are numerous books written by sufferers of various kinds and, compared with a previous generation, we are much more aware of their difficulties. Television, too, with its honest interviews and documentaries has done much to enlighten us concerning those members of society who suffer.

I have seen very few books which are written for ordinary members of the public on the subject of dyslexia. I therefore commend this book to you in the hope that it will enable you to form genuine friendships with the many Mike Rydens of this world.

Derek Copley

Acknowledgements

Thank you to all who have considered my work for its substance rather than condemning or shunning me for my lack of reading ability. I am ever more grateful to those who have accepted my shortcomings and have helped me by reading to me in a non-condescending fashion. They gave me the confidence to keep trying to learn how to cope and how to circumvent the written word.

Special thanks to my family for their support and patience in my studies and career.

Finally, thanks to all who do not judge someone on first impressions, whatever the problem, before they know the abilities or the shortcomings of the person concerned.

Michael Ryden

Give Me a Chance

by Mike Ryden – a dyslexic

Do I smell because I cannot read?

Socially they rebuff me, maybe because they don't know how to handle it themselves and it seems especially hard to share the good things in life. If you can't read, you are by implication stupid and therefore not worth bothering with.

I ask you, is reading so all important? Believe me, it is certainly hard not being able to read – but is it the only way to communicate?

Would you ask a blind person to look at a photograph, or take a deaf person to an orchestral concert?

So why disregard me as useless because I cannot read?

Can you do everything?

Give me a fair chance – a fair one is all I ask for, no more, no less.

Accept me for the person I am, and for the things that I can do.

Are any of us perfect?

PART I

What is Dyslexia?

A fundamental part of life is about communication. Good communication is the art of allowing the recipient to understand the intended message regardless of its form or format. It is the obligation of a good communicator to convey the message in the appropriate format, rather than the recipient trying to guess the desired message.

The *Merck Manual* defines dyslexia as "a distinct reading problem based on specific deficiencies or deficits in phonologic processing present from birth, which affect word learning and which may also cause language disabilities. It is also described as a disorder that interferes with learning to read, despite average or above-average intelligence, adequate motivation and educational opportunities, socioeconomic advantage, and sensory acuity within normal limits."

From *The Merck Manual of Diagnosis and Therapy*, Edition 16, p.2105, edited by Robert Berkow. Copyright 1992 by Merck & Co., Inc., Rahway, NJ. Used with permission.

Introduction

In today's society one's whole life style is based on reading — from finding street directions and shopping, to checking what is on the TV or radio, and trying to keep up with local and world news.

In the workplace, there is now an excessive amount of paperwork and many forms to be dealt with — even where manual jobs which really require no literacy skills are concerned. One's ability to fill in forms seems to be the yardstick, rather than one's ability to perform the task.

Is the processing of a form a measure of intelligence?

This book is by no means intended to be an an in-depth study of the causes of and possible treatments for learning difficulties, but is intended to create an awareness of the experience of dyslexia — taken from the experience of some other dyslexics as well as my own.

My aim is to cultivate the attitudes of all who may come in contact with the dyslexic including parents, teachers and employers. They will be provided with the information necessary to gain insight into understanding a dyslexic's strengths as well as to minimise the effects of the dyslexia.

There are various ways and means of both testing and teaching the dyslexic which require a minimum of effort from teachers, employers and governing bodies.

For example, it is not necessary to write an essay to test a manual skill, and in a workshop, the student may do an exemplary job even though he or she is unable to give an explanation of the process in writing.

Many people can write a beautiful essay, but are unable to physically perform what they have written out. Most dyslexics are quite the opposite – performing well, but not reading or writing "adequately".

*   *   *

What is Dyslexia?

Although the centre of the thought system of the dyslexic is functioning well in most cases, the ability of one or both of the input (obtaining information) or output (imparting information) modes is impaired in some way.

COMMUNICATING – the problem is to find a form or method of communication that is accessible to all parties concerned, and that results in the least impairment or distortion of information. This method, by implication, will be the one that is most efficient.

TESTING – where it is possible to give a person tests or examinations in the mode (information format) that best re-creates the working environment, such a test provides a far more realistic assessment of their skills than would a purely written evaluation.

In a woodwork class, for example, give the student a joint to make, and ask him or her to just include short notes where absolutely necessary, rather than asking for the task to be described in essay form. Then grade them on their grammar.

*   *   *

It is estimated that over 10% of the population suffers from dyslexia to some extent, and that about four people in every hundred need special help.

Dyslexia is a genuine difficulty that occurs irrespective of intelligence or social standing. The problems it causes can largely be overcome by the right teaching, understanding, encouragement and support for the dyslexic. However, it is paramount that their drive is nurtured to the level where they themselves will gain the confidence to overcome the handicap in all of their endeavours.

It is not possible for a layman to give advice on the diagnosis and treatment of dyslexia. But with the knowledge of how dyslexia affects some dyslexics one can have enough empathy to enable a person to find strategies to assist them in their endeavours. The following section is intended to give some general indication of how dyslexia may show itself.

*   *   *

Recognising Dyslexia

Dyslexia can show itself in many ways, including the following:

In writing and reading

- poor concentration or inaccuracy in reading and spelling

- a tendency to put letters or figures the wrong way round, and to reverse their order (for example, b for d, 6 for 9, 48 for 84, raw for war)

- reading a word correctly and then failing to recognise it further down the page

- ability to answer questions orally, but difficulty in writing down the answer

- spelling the same word in several different ways without recognising the correct spelling

- difficulty in copying written work

- difficulty in taking notes

- difficulty in understanding time and tense

- difficulty in working with serial numbering.

In other ways

- being bright in many ways but with an apparent block in others

- confusing left and right

- ambidexterity

- difficulty in carrying out a sequence of instructions

- unusual clumsiness or poor co-ordination

- hyperactivity or disruptive behaviour, particularly in a learning situation

- difficulty in getting sequences in the right order, such as months of the year, or the alphabet.

Characteristics

Many dyslexic children display more than one of the following characteristics:

- hyperactive

- needs less sleep than the average child

- easily distracted (possibly seeing too much all at once
  rather than not paying attention)

- untidy and disorganised

- poor motor co-ordination

- tendency toward depression

- a loner.

*   *   *

It is a great relief when the problem is diagnosed and the
child not only knows that he or she is not the only one with
this problem, but also knows that what is causing the
trouble actually has a name.

Try to imagine yourself accomplishing everyday tasks
without the skills which you take for granted.

It is important to remember that these characteristics are not necessarily indicative of dyslexia, and that a professional diagnosis should be sought.

*   *   *

It is important to have professional advice as soon as possible, and this should be available through the Local Education Authorities (LEAs). Under the 1981 Education Act children with special needs should, in theory, get appropriate help – in practice, only two or three LEAs provide properly trained teachers for dyslexics. LEAs can assess, but it is unlikely that schools will offer appropriate teaching – and remedial teaching is not sufficient. The teacher must be trained in dyslexia and multi-sensory techniques. The majority of parents still have to resort to private teachers. The earlier that help is given, the better the chance of success in minimising the effects of dyslexia.

Within guidelines, the children should be allowed to make their own decisions as far and as early as possible, because it will become more difficult for them to rely on outside help as they get older. With age, also, comes embarrassment at still not being able to read.

PART II

How Does it Feel?

This section provides examples of just how distorted written information can become to a dyslexic.

To gain a full appreciation of the next section it is imperative to cover the bottom section as you take the test. As you read each passage give yourself three or four minutes to comprehend the meaning. For best results, get someone else to quiz you on your comprehension of the passage. You will realise that effort alone is not enough to overcome the problem.

Text used is about a river trip — written by the author of this book and subsequently published.

Concept Reversal

It will been nearly one hundred and twenty days before Minor John Wesley Powell broak history sell follerwing an experdition around the cataract of the Small Canyon. Faced apart seemingly easy evens – some physical, none supernatural – Powell challenged the Colorado flow…

— — — — — — — — — — — — — — — — — — —

It has been almost one hundred and twenty years since Major John Powell made history by leading an expedition through the cataract of the Grand Canyon. Faced with seemingly insurmountable odds – some physical, some natural – Powell challenged the Colorado river…

Sometimes a dyslexic will perceive the meaning of a word or phrase as its exact opposite.

Vertical Disorientation

anddshe was eqAlly adeht at rafting in rhe gad le boat. ulong sitp ynn, onother pataplegic preeg lwho hrsfthe uwe ofLonly ane arm)and sevgra(othea reinds n they pfddle adroitlt theough eiery sapid a,d went aor the big wayer whrrever vt war.

— — — — — — — — — — — — — — — — — —

and she was equally adept at rafting in the paddle boat. Along with Lynn, another paraplegic Gregg (who has the use of only one arm) and several other friends, they paddled adroitly through every rapid and went for the big water wherever it was.

Letters, or whole words, may appear to be in the line above or below.

Lateral Disorientation

humand spirof intere.test Wef ita nda namileWh culties mustdiff havef acquestuion eth haveseds noe toram ithw ,allenchedynolgni ot mrnaun ethe all dame tedlyuod saw eatrg casueeb rmoe eth tunforateun ciCivel raW sihaof diccanet.

---

a test of human spirit and integrity. While few question the difficulties he must have faced having only one arm to work with, the challenge undoubtedly was made all the more great because of his unfortunate Civil War accident.

Here words or parts of words appear in the wrong place - sometimes the letters appearing in reverse order - along a line.

Fading

af er the oats e e pul ed as ore for unch or f r t e nigh ,
the w ee chairs   ere un oa ed f rst so h students c   ld
take   re of set in   up ten s and   et ing into d y clot es.

——— — — — — — — — — — — — — —

after the boats were pulled ashore for lunch or for the night,
the wheelchairs were unloaded first so the students could
take care of setting up tents and getting into dry clothes.

*The first few letters may seem clear and then others
fade until they are barely discernible. This is random
fading, appearing as anything between 20 and 100
dot (full black).*

Mirror Image

On the San Juan river in southern Utah just a few months ago, a special group of NAU students faced a challenge equally as great. Six eager and energetic disabled students, five relying on wheelchairs for their primary means of locomotion, participated in a weekend river trip of

- - - - - - - - - - - - - - - - - - -

On the San Juan river in southern Utah just a few months ago, a special group of NAU students faced a challenge equally as great. Six eager and energetic disabled students, five relying on wheelchairs for their primary means of locomotion, participated in a weekend river trip of

Text may appear completely reversed, as though it were being seen in a mirror.

Omitting Letters

apoxmately thity mles bteen Bluff and Mexcan Ht, Utah. Althogh the San Jan has been mpped and the eqipmnt hs impved sine Pwells adeture, for thse studnts, the adenture ws no lss grat.

— — — — — — — — — — — — — — — — — —

approximately thirty miles between Bluff and Mexican Hat, Utah. Although the San Juan has been mapped and the equipment has improved since Powell's adventure, for these students, the adventure was no less great.

Random letters may be omitted.

Omitting Words (Telegraph Style)

It not been that diabled people oppertunity explore remote wild. Prejudice attertuides responsibility barries people willing risk adventure progressive administrators

— — — — — — — — — — — — — — — —

It has not been long that disabled people have had the opportunity to explore and enjoy remote wild areas. Prejudice and attitudes about responsibility have served as barriers to these people who are willing to take risks and enjoy adventure. But progressive administrators like Linda Price

Whole words may be omitted, leaving only the key words.

Omitting Key Words

Student services at the, and AL director of Educational Program, are all that. With the of people like of Flagstaff Parks and Department and of the river trip are changing and are relizing.

— — — — — — — — — — — — — — — — —

Disabled Student Services at the university, and Al Jamieson, director of NAU's Educational Support Program, are changing all that. With the help of people like Mark Grant of the Flagstaff Parks and Recreation Department and leader of the trip, attitudes are changing and people are realising

---

Key words may be omitted.

Inversions

that the four-walled classroom is not the limit to education. The spirit and integrity of the students who participate in this trip is unrivalled to any yet witnessed. Helen, head cook for the trip, prepared an elegant menu – steak, oysters, shrimp omelettes

— — — — — — — — — — — — — — —

that the four-walled classroom is not the limit to education. The spirit and integrity of the students who participate in this trip is unrivalled to any yet witnessed. Helen, head cook for the trip, prepared an elegant menu – steak, oysters, shrimp omelettes

Text may actually appear to be upside down.

Horizontal Reversal

In order to have some idea of the problem PLEASE take two or three minutes to try the following experiment.

Hold a mirror at eye level reflecting double lined shapes. Looking ONLY through the mirror draw a line between the existing ones, using all three shapes.

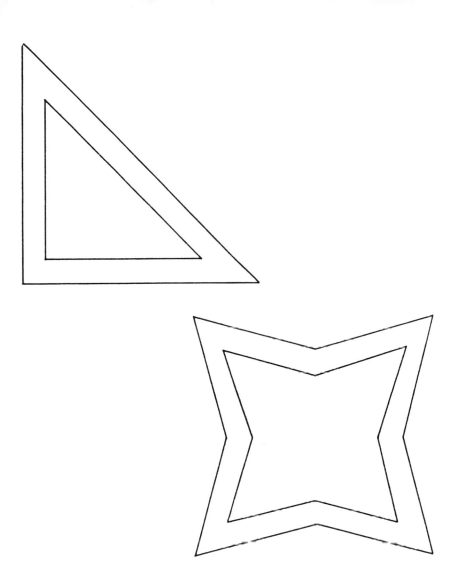

Having finished this experiment you may now have some indication of the feelings of frustration felt by many dyslexics who actually do see things in this way some of the time.

Words and Symbols

Play la crosse hear

The words describing familiar symbols may appear meaningless, or have quite a different meaning which can cause some catastrophic results.

PART III

Attitudes, Counselling and Teaching

Barriers to Learning

- Not having ready access to information. (Looking words up in a dictionary is fine if you can make an educated guess at approximately the correct spelling in the first place.)

- Lack of technical knowledge. (Compensatory knowledge and general knowledge can be a result of reading problems.)

- Inability to express to others the exact nature of the problem.

- Inappropriate learning environment.

- Inappropriate evaluation of effort and work.

- Avoidance of teachers and social occasions where reading skills are needed.

- Focusing on disabilities rather than abilities.

- As others cannot see an immediate problem they assume that one does not exist, and therefore find it very hard to identify or imagine the difficulties involved.

- Lack of confidence and low self-esteem, causing both the pupil and the teacher to have poor expectations – thus paving the way for failure rather than for success.

Commonly Recurring Attitudes

From teachers and peers:

- Inferior *(why should I invest my time in them?)*

- Thick *(Give up, you'll never make it)*

- Slow *(take your time, you will understand it eventually)*

- Mentally ill *(because you cannot understand in this particular format)*

- Incorrect *(retribution)*

- Lazy *(just try harder and you will overcome it)*

- Not interested *(otherwise they would want to read it)*.

Learning disabled versus peers

- Better orally

- Good conceptual memory

- Misuse of words

- Distractive techniques are commonly employed by the learning disabled

- Slow to answer – even though knowing the answer

- *Forgetting* homework (to avoid humiliation)

- Taking *the easy way out* (Why bother after repetitive failures?)

- Pretending to be *dumb* and therefore left alone

- *Class clown* (a mask for the real pain).

Feelings

- Absolutely frustrated with the inability to get through to others coherently – sense of inadequacy

- Wanting to give up

- Angry – furious to the point where sequential thought breaks up at random

- Want to get physically aggressive towards teachers and others

- Having to fight back all the time

- Unfair – persecuted – always being on the defensive

- Isolation – totally and utterly alone

- Rushed – panic

- Escape to an area of ability

- Maybe I am stupid after all (despite a fairly high IQ)?

- Is it worth it all?

- Total Despair

Finally, to move forward, there must be

- Acceptance of one's disability

- Recognition and use of one's abilities

- Recognition of their innate value as a person.

*   *   *

There is little stability in a dyslexic's world, for not only the severity but also the form of their problems alter on a daily basis. There is a tremendous number of symbols which we are all exposed to daily which dyslexics cannot always fully understand. This further adds to their confusion and frustration and increases their problems.

It has been shown that many dyslexic students can understand words just as well if they hold the text at right angles or even upside down, as though the shape of the word is more important than the letters.

Statements Made by Dyslexics

My hands don't do what my brain tells them to.

My brain will not always do what I want it to.

It is impossible to write down what I am thinking – it comes out wrong.

Some days I can read reasonably well – other days not at all.

I can only manage to read for short periods.

I feel completely exhausted when I have read something.

Although I have read it, I have no comprehension of what it was.

*   *   *

There seems to be a connection which is especially strong in dyslexics, whereby stress, health and the emotions have a direct bearing on reading ability. Even when a dyslexic has achieved great progress, stress, fatigue, or a particular emotional state can have a temporary effect on the quality of written work.

A Common Social Situation

The dyslexic meets a stranger or is involved with a person who has no knowledge of dyslexic problems. The dyslexic feels inadequate and apprehensive and thus withdraws. This is followed by rejection on both sides.

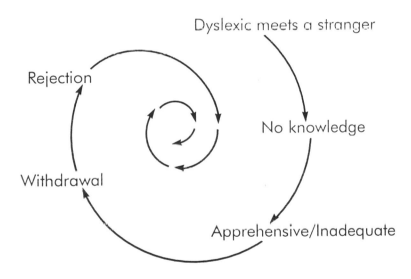

This spiral forces many dyslexics to become "LONERS" and therefore to feel very isolated. This scenario is a contributing factor to low self-esteem and can lead to depression.

Counselling Dyslexia

A counsellor faced with a person who displays:

- Disorderly conduct

- Inappropriate behaviour

- Acting up

- Low self-esteem and/or depression

would:

(a) Find out what the source of their anger, frustration, and hostility is.

(b) Teach appropriate coping strategies to replace the inappropriate ones (i.e. acting-out behaviour).

Q. How would you handle the client?

A. Ask what the specific problems are. Listen with empathy, and try to understand the underlying emotions. Become more aware of their disabilities through research. Help them to understand and cope with their problems and inherent disabilities.

Q. How would you want others to respond to them?

A. They should be aware of the problem but treat the dyslexic as they would any other person.
They should focus on the dyslexic's abilities and capitalise on those.

Q. What would you do with the released emotions related to the problem?

A. Encourage the person to develop their abilities, thus increasing their self-confidence (focusing on other things). Teach the person how to accept their frustrations and redirect their energies.

Advice for teaching and learning

- See that the teacher is made aware of the person who has the problem, preferably by a person of authority as well as by the student him or herself.

- Find the best mode of learning for that student.

- Explore different formats for testing (i.e. verbal input/output, diagrammatically, or even manually).

Teaching

It is most useful for a student to be able to select — from information available at the advice centre — the teacher whose method of teaching is most compatible with the student's mode of learning.

This can be achieved by inquiring with which mode a teacher usually conveys information to the students.

This should relieve some of the stresses on both teachers and students caused by the lack of appropriate communication, and thus create a far more efficient educational system for the dyslexic.

Practical Help

- Allow tape recorders in classes — particularly lectures; also let them be used on homework assignments.

- Encourage the use of computers; they are now a normal part of life.

Writing

Computers and word processors are most useful instruments for the dyslexic, for once they have got the bulk of the text programmed into the machine, it can be edited and organised by a non-dyslexic if necessary, and then retrieved again as and when required by the dyslexic. This is far more helpful than the old method of repetitive rewriting which continuously created more and more mistakes and the inevitable frustrations.

However, the spell checker (with or without the computer) is similar to a dictionary, where one must know either the approximate or the phonetic spelling. A dyslexic frequently cannot differentiate between slightly different spellings of words which would not be discovered by using a spell checker.

In assessing their work one should check for the intent of the piece rather than the literal use of the words (e.g. a few words may be spelled incorrectly yet the work has good content).

Note taking

The ability to take notes is a necessary skill for life, and it is paramount that a person develops their own format, sometimes helped and guided by others. It is critical that he or she be allowed to pick out what is important and what *memory joggers* are useful to them rather than to teachers or others concerned.

For example, the study notes must be precise and in a logical sequence for the learning disabled to grasp, and need to be checked for accuracy of content, rather than for the layout and format of the notes – dyslexics cannot check for themselves as preconceptions can, and frequently do, come into play.

Time and effort

While teaching the correct use and management of time is very important to enable the student to achieve effective output of work, an element of constant encouragement should be given. Unless there is some form of recognition of EFFORT as well as achievement, the student will unquestionably be tempted to neglect those subjects in which they consistently receive zero response.

Communication of ideas

Mere repetition is not necessarily useful in the explanation of a concept or idea in the form in which it was first presented – it may be better to approach from a different angle which the dyslexic may more readily understand. For example, an auditory learner may not be able to read and understand written concepts at all, so written repetition would be useless, and a few extra minutes taken at this time may help to solve the problem of communication – and thus save valuable time in correcting mistakes and misun-derstandings.

After all, one would not attempt to teach a blind student solely from the blackboard, so why a dyslexic? While the teacher is writing the question, it should also be read out loud.

In business it may be more beneficial to all, in the long term, to explain an instruction directly, rather than leave a dyslexic to read and work it out for themselves, as many serious mistakes can be caused by the misunderstanding or reversal of a single word or phrase. Once the concept is grasped, often the dyslexic is very good at the intuitive use and interpretation of the instructions.

For the dyslexic there cannot be too much emphasis on

- tell

- demonstrate

- list key concepts

- question to assess correct intake

- and also on allowing the learner to tell, demonstrate, repeat key concepts and practice.

Learning

There must exist a strong desire to learn, especially in the older student, and it is important that the content of the books and articles used be of interest to the age group and individual concerned. There is nothing more humiliating for a ten-year-old than to be given a reader for five-year-olds about the cat sitting on the mat.

If books can be related to the student's interest in sport or a hobby, for example, it will help to keep them involved with reading outside school hours, and provide great motivation.

Probably the most useful fact which dyslexics should be made aware of is that life is not fair, and that they will just have to work that much harder and persevere that much more than the average person, to obtain results comparable with those of people without handicaps.

This awareness will be necessary as the dyslexic gets older, and will be essential – together with the extra drive needed – to compete successfully in the workplace.

*   *   *

Appendices

History of Dyslexia

It appears that dyslexia was first diagnosed in 1895 by Dr James Hinshelwood from Glasgow. He stated that a "very intelligent boy of twelve was unable to learn to read, but had all the lessons in the class been oral lessons, he would probably have been the brightest boy."

In 1924 – Dr Samuel Orton, an American neuropsychiatrist, began research backed by the Rockefeller Foundation.

In November 1979 – an article in the Boston Globe publicised neurological research work at the Beth Israel Hospital which claimed discovery of physical evidence which showed distinct abnormalities in brain cell structure. This was the work of Dr Anthony Galaburda and Dr Thomas Kemper, neurologists at Beth Israel.

In 1988 – for the first time ever, a student was allowed to use a word processor to take a GCSE examination (*Daily Express, 13th June 1988*)

Experts seem to give various reasons (somewhat unconvincingly) as to why there has been such scant correlation between the educational and neurological fields, and it is to be hoped that, in the light of new discoveries, this particular situation will improve rapidly.

People

Some of the well-known people who have succeeded in their chosen careers in spite of their learning disability problems:

Thomas Edison: Thought mentally slow by his teacher, he was withdrawn from school and taught by his mother. He later invented the electric light bulb and the phonograph.

Albert Einstein: Teachers considered him to be mentally slow, unsociable and a "dreamer". Failed first college entrance examinations, and in the two years after graduation he obtained (and lost!) three teaching positions.

Ultimately he developed the theory of relativity.

Paul Erlich (1854–1915): Completely inept at examinations, he was excused composition writing in college and his thesis was written by a scribe.

He became a famous German bacteriologist, and won a Nobel prize.

Susan Hampshire: Leading stage and screen actress who has appeared on television programmes about dyslexia.

William James: The first American psychologist: He wrote in his book *The Principles of Psychology*, "I am myself a very poor visualiser and find that I can seldom call to mind a single alphabet letter purely in retinal terms. I must trace the letter by running my mental eye over its contour in order that the image of it shall leave any distinctness at all."

He was a famous educational psychologist and if the principles that he expressed in his "talks to teachers on psychology" were followed, many dyslexic students would have little difficulty in capitalising on their abilities, or in learning.

George Patton: He could not read by the age of 12, and remained deficient in reading all his life. He had, however, an excellent memory and became a famous World War II Five Star General. This was partly due to his memory but also his unorthodox and innovative battle strategies.

Nelson Rockefeller: Became vice president of the U.S.A.

Auguste Rodin: Became a pupil of the Jesuit school at which he was educated. An earlier tutor wrote to his father "He is ineducable. The sooner you put him to work the better."

He sculpted the classic statue "The Thinker".

George Washington: At the age of fourteen, his grammar and spelling was atrocious, but he had a flair for mathematics.

He became a "Gentleman Farmer" and President of a new nation, the U.S.A.

Woodrow Wilson: Unable to read the alphabet at the age of nine. He was eleven when he learned to read.

He also became a president of the U.S.A.

*   *   *

These are just a few of the people who "made it" and they have demonstrated that it is possible despite all the odds against them – they obviously must have had great determination.

So how many people might there be, who with a little patient encouragement, might well make worthwhile contributions to the scientific, economic or artistic fields – and to society as a whole?

What will be your role in the success or hindrance of the next dyslexic you meet?

Books

Spelling Made Easy
V. Brand
Egon Publications, Baldock, 1984
(A series of titles for different age groups)

Development of Dyslexia
Macdonald Critchley
Heinemann, London, 1964

The British Ability Scales
C.D. Elliott and D.J. Murray
NFER-Nelson, Windsor, 1983

Overcoming Dyslexia
B. Hornsby
Macdonald, London, 1984

Help for Dyslexic Children
T.R. Miles and E. Miles
Methuen, London, 1983

Understanding Dyslexia
T.R. Miles and E. Miles
Better Books, Bath, 1986

Check-Mate
A Pocket-Sized Guide to Everyday Spellings for Dyslexics
Alan O'Brien
Jessica Kingsley Publishers, London, 1993

Children with Special Needs
Assessment, Law and Practice – Caught in the Acts, 3rd edition
John Friel
Jessica Kingsley Publishers, London, 1995

Signposts to Spelling
J. Pollock
Helen Arkell Dyslexia Centre, London, 1978

The School Daze of the Learning Disability Child
W. Silva
Alpern Communications,
220 Gulph Hills Road,
Radnor, PA 19087, U.S.A.

Help for Dyslexic Adults
E.G. Stirling
Better Books, Bath, 1985
(Better Books catalogue contains many useful titles and learning aides and software for Spectrum and BBC 'B')

Journals

Learning Disability Journal (published quarterly)
Department of Special Education
435 Herbert C. Miller Building
University of Kansas Medical Center
Kansas City, KS 66103

Journal of Learning Disabilities
Professional Press
5 N Wabash Avenue
Chicago, IL 60602

(Ask at your local reference library for other books)

Useful Addresses
United Kingdom

Adult Dyslexia Organisation
336 Brixton Road
London SW9
Tel: (0171) 924 9559

Advisory Centre for Education (ACE)
1b Aberdeen Studios
22–24 Highbury Grove
London N5 2DQ
Tel: (0171) 354 8321

British Dyslexia Association
98 London Road
Reading
Berkshire RG1 5AU
Tel: (01734) 668271/2

(A mine of further help and information. Local associations throughout the country – list of addresses available from B.D.A. The Association holds meetings several times a year.)

Dyslexia Institute
133 Gresham Road
Staines
Middlesex TW18 2AJ
Tel: (01784) 463851

Helen Arkell Dyslexia Centre
17 Wandsworth Common West Side
London SW18 2ED
Tel: (0181) 871 2846

Learning Development Aids
Duke Street
Wisbech
Cambridgeshire PE13 2AE
Tel. (01945) 463441
(also do lots of books, educational packs, games, software, etc.)

Parents Advice Line
(run by the journal *Special Children*)
Box 161
Rode
Bath
Tel: (0898) 333001

Many universities now have a department covering Learning Disabilities. They have access to a great deal of information and I have found them to be most helpful.

Useful Addresses
U S A

ACLD (Advisory Center for Learning Disability)
5225 Grace Street
Pittsburgh, PA 15236

The Orton Dyslexia Society
Chester Bldg., Ste. 382
8600 La Salle Road
Baltimore, MD 21286–2044

Xerox Kurzweil Personal Reader – optical scanner
that turns print into speech – weighs less than 20 lbs and
speech rate is from 120 words to 350 words per minute.
185 Albany Street, Cambridge, MA 02139
Tel: (800) 343 0311

About the Author

Michael V. Ryden – born 4th April 1960

Diagnosed as dyslexic by McDonald Critchley (London) in 1969, and then examined by an educational psychologist who reported an IQ rating of well above average. A further test in 1973 confirmed this.

The only help that the local education authority was able to offer at that time was a suggestion that he be sent to a school for the educationally subnormal, as they had no special help available and in fact questioned whether such a thing as dyslexia existed.

After a lot of effort and help he obtained three CSEs, seven GSEs and two GCE 'A' Level grades in examinations, GSE grade four being the highest in English and Maths and Physics being taken at 'A' Level.

He took a course in Business Studies and learned a great deal although he failed the final examinations because of poor English grades.

He could not gain entrance to any university in the United Kingdom because of his English grades. However, he was fortunate enough to go to a university in the United States of America where he was frequently on the "Dean's List" and even on the "National Dean's List". He graduated with a Bachelor of Science degree in Photography and Graphics.

He is now a developer in Colorado and also gives lectures on Dyslexia.